Network for a Job
The PeopleHirePeople®
process to build a job-
specific network.

Kathleen Conners

Contents

Introduction

Dear Job Candidate,

You need a job! You perfected your resume, interviewing and negotiating skills. You applied online and contacted friends, family and colleagues. You engaged in elevator speeches and career informational interviews. Your problem is no interviews and no job offers!

Using the process in this guide, you can discover how effective networking leads to private firsthand information and job referrals that will get you hired.

The PeopleHirePeople® process introduces you to professionals you need to know to get a job!

To build your job specific network you will learn how to find these professionals. You will initiate conversations employing "common connectors". You will easily engage in networking conversations asking key questions. You will discover private firsthand information for referrals to unadvertised jobs.

Over two decades of recruitment and job development, I still find my best candidates through networked referrals. When I do not have a single contact to begin a candidate search, I determine which professionals I need to contact. These professionals have established networks containing the types of individuals I need to fill positions. My network contacts share private firsthand information and great referrals invaluable to my successful career in job placement.

This PeopleHirePeople® process will work for you.

Discover how great networkers get great job offers. Network On!

Kathleen Conners

Hunt by the Numbers

Does your job hunt follow the numbers?

We are an information society that devours statistics. We use stats for investing, purchasing, betting, voting, dieting and just about everything in our daily lives.

It's a numbers game. The more resumes you get out, the better your employment chances, right? Not necessarily. You must evaluate what activities deliver the best return on your time, effort and expense. If you are motivated by statistics, you will appreciate the following stats.

5% of job candidates obtain employment through Internet job boards. Yet the number one job-seeking activity is sending out hundreds of resumes in response to Internet job postings.

15% of job candidates find employment opportunities through recruiters.

65 to 70% of jobs are created by small businesses. Most do not advertise positions. In addition, small, private businesses are harder to find as they are often not listed in published databases. However, it's worth noting that small businesses add employees before larger companies do during an economic recovery, according to *Money Magazine* (April 2010, page 18).

70% to 85% of candidates obtain employment through networking. All career professionals agree on the importance of networking. When asked how they obtain their best jobs, most professionals answered via personal referrals through their networks.

85% of jobs are never advertised. Posted Internet and advertised jobs are mainly for large corporations with big advertising and human resource budgets.

90% of hiring managers find candidates through their own contacts in some way. Hiring managers are more inclined to hire through referrals from employees, colleagues, professional associates or recruiters than from a stack of resumes delivered by human resources.

Here is what the numbers indicate you need to do to get a job.

One: Spend the least amount of time on job boards and online applications.

Two: Focus your effort on small businesses that are not advertising employment opportunities.
Three: Think quality over quantity and create one-on-one industry contacts.

The old expression "numbers count" applies to job hunting. Create positive results with the numbers that really matter and adjust your job hunting strategies accordingly.

Get Interviews and Job Offers

As statistics demonstrate, successful job hunts are network driven. Straightforward, commonsense networking uncovers employment opportunities. Only by engaging in quality one-on-one real people conversations will you acquire essential firsthand information that will help you obtain a job, information that cannot be found through research alone.

This guide will help you create an effective job network. Learn how to connect and converse with professionals you need to know to get a job. Determine common connectors for growing your job network. Discover the art of asking those crucial questions to get the answers and referrals that are critical to success. Learn how to network to beat your competition for employment.

Employ PeopleHirePeople®'s three-step process to build a job specific network:

Who to Contact: Identify professionals with vast networks.

How to Hunt: Investigate how to find these professionals.

What to Ask: Initiate questions for job information and referrals.

# ✔ Who to Contact

Section A:
Who to Contact

This section identifies three key contacts you need to know because they are people in the know: sales professionals, industry analysts and contingency/retained recruiters. The common denominator for these contacts is that each has a vast current industry network by the very nature of their employment. They have access to information you won't find on the Internet or in the media.

Chapter 1: Sales Professional Contacts

Why Contact Sales Professionals?

Good sales professionals know what is happening in industry. They are aware of industry startups, award winners, growth companies, funding recipients and competitors. What's more, sales professionals acquire industry information and maintain contact with real people within companies every single day. You can quickly gain the most up-to-date industry knowledge and referrals by tapping into their networks.

Sales professionals often know about jobs becoming available within their company because they have firsthand knowledge of increased sales of their company's products or services. In order to service the increased sales growth, sales professionals can forecast the need for hiring. They also have direct relationships with hiring managers. Sales people expand their network daily through referrals and you would be wise to follow their techniques if you are looking to grow your job network. A sales professional's list of customers can be a great starting point.

Boots on the Ground

While technology provides many advantages in modern war, it's "boots on the ground" that make it possible to win wars. Army commanders listen to foot soldiers for updated intelligence. You need to do the same with your own "boots on the ground": industry sales professionals.

Sales professionals have a tremendous existing network and are always in growth mode to find new customers and markets. Many will have current information since they literally knock on doors and speak to their clients directly. If you're savvy enough, you can tap these pavement pounders for firsthand, exclusive industry information.

Whether a company is hiring or firing is not always publicized. Sales professionals often have that insider knowledge. They have also been known to keep on file employee resumes from companies that have purchased their products. People often confidentially ask salespeople to keep them posted on jobs outside of their current employment.

Getting information firsthand can help you use your time wisely. A company once contacted me to find a highly specialized engineer. I submitted the details of a couple of qualified candidates, but the hiring manager was unresponsive. I engaged the company's salesperson in conversation, asking key questions. The salesperson told me that the company currently had forty-nine employees and the owners would not be hiring due to legal regulations. Expanding the number of employees to fifty or more would become too costly. Although the company website continued to display several job descriptions on its career page, insider information told a different story and I stopped efforts to find candidates for this company.

Ask the right questions and sales professionals will share information with you. Assistance may vary from providing details of unadvertised jobs to direct referrals to hiring managers. Ask key probing questions: Which companies have recently purchased the product you sell? Which of your customers is expanding? Who would be good contacts within your customer companies? Have you recently called on any new startup companies?

Not every company has their own sales force. Some products and services are sold through value-added resellers (VAR) or preferred resellers. A VAR adds features or services to an existing product then resells it (usually to end-users) as an integrated product or complete "turn-key" solution. VARs also hold complementary seminars or workshops for the various products they sell.

Obtaining direct referrals from those who possess established networks is how you transition from candidate to employee. Tapping into established, well-connected industry networks is also time efficient. You will find that industry sales professionals make terrific additions to your job network.

How to Hunt Sales Professionals

Action #1
Make a list of all products, services and equipment that would be used for your position of interest. If you are in a management role, list items your employees use. For new graduates, make a list that you would use on the job.

Action #2
Gather business cards and compile a list of all the vendors who have called on you in the past to sell their products and services. Contact each vendor/salesperson. If they are no longer in the

position, ask for details of the person now in the role and call that individual.

Action #3

Research the producer, creator or manufacturer for the product, service or tool. Call companies to determine whether they sell their own products or have other entities that sell their products, such as value-added resellers (VAR) or preferred resellers. Ask for the sales professional who covers the geographic area of your interest, whether this is where you currently live or where you would prefer to relocate.

PeoplePoints

New Graduates: Start your job network with several industry salespeople. This will take you outside your comfort zone, but it is a great starting point for referrals. Sales professionals can be the easiest people with whom to start and facilitate conversations. If you are unfamiliar with the tools of your new profession, ask your college professors and industry professionals to assist with compiling a list. Contact university alumni to find out about the tools of the industry.

Experienced Professionals: When your network needs a jumpstart, make contacting salespeople your priority. Connecting with sales professionals gives your existing network a super boost and provides you with current information. If you have not recently used or purchased relevant industry tools, it's a good idea to make a list of the ones you used at your last company. Perhaps ask a former manager for his or her purchasing history and start from there.

Chapter 2: Industry Analyst Contacts

Why Contact Industry Analysts?

Industry analysts perform market research within a particular industry segment. They differ from financial analysts whose focus is on equities, investments or financial opportunities. Analyst firms offer their clients consultative services, independent advice and research for purchases, suppliers, and management and deployment strategies.

Industry analysts perform primary and secondary market research. They make forecasts or predictions, or expound on mergers/acquisitions. Analysts usually work for research and advisory services firms while some also perform advisory and consulting services.

Analysts are active in industry in many ways, from speaking at or moderating events, to authoring articles in industry publications, to delivering custom research for consulting projects. Industry analysts contact hundreds of companies a year to do their research. Analysts have tremendous networks because of the nature of their positions. Not only can they recommend industry companies, but they interact with C-level managers and executive management, and can also identify specific contacts within those companies.

Super Sources

When contacted by experienced telecom candidate Tim, I asked him, "So what would you like to do when you grow up?" "That's an interesting question that no one in the past thirty years has ever asked me," he replied. "I'm searching for a C-level position or above." When Tim added that the most interesting aspect of his work experience had been making presentations to analysts, my next question was, "Have you spoken with any industry analysts for job referrals?" No, he had not.

I told Tim about a return trip from delivering a PeopleHirePeople® lecture at a Texas university. In conversation with a gentleman seated next to me on the plane, he revealed he was a former industry analyst. On hearing how I instruct job candidates to contact analysts for job leads he said this advice was entirely on the mark. In fact, in his position as an analyst, he had frequently put executives in touch with their future employees. Introductions had been made on his behalf numerous times and he had made many employment matches at all levels.

As key questions are always part of PeopleHirePeople® conversations, I asked him what he was doing now he was no longer an analyst. He had started a firm to instruct marketing departments within companies on how to contact and interact directly with analysts. Thus, this eliminated the practice of hiring PR firms to make connections at a large expense.

Tim had an "a-ha moment" once he heard this tale. It never occurred to him to contact analysts. He quickly recalled former analyst connections he had forgotten and he understood where to hunt new analyst contacts. Tim realized that industry analysts would make fantastic sources for introductions to key industry contacts and employment opportunities.

A second candidate, James, told me, "I want to get back to the auto industry and Detroit." James had been away from the Detroit auto industry for more than a decade and was now seeking to return in a senior level position. He was counting on his few contacts in the Ford Motor Company to assist him with his job hunt.

James felt stuck and did not know how to go about getting any other industry leads.

I pointed out that there should be many more opportunities other than Ford and the other major auto manufacturers, such as GM and Chrysler. For example, had James considered contacting any of the suppliers to these companies?

A first step for James was to research current auto industry information. From this initial research, it was possible to find several auto industry analysts who might provide good quality information. The next step would be to make contact with specific analysts within those companies.

An online search with the keywords "automotive", "industry" and "analyst" revealed two companies of interest: IHS and Ernst & Young. IHS' website listed the names and bios of more than half a dozen automotive analysts. A search of the Ernst & Young website revealed details of its Global Automotive Center as well as the fact that the company audit 34% of the Forbes Global 2000 automotive sector companies. Both websites were great sources of the most up-to-date industry information and people connections.

There will be analysts that are responsive and others that won't be, as in all networking. For any one contact that is inaccessible, you will find an analyst with whom to converse.

How to Hunt Industry Analysts

Action #1
Use a search engine and enter keywords related to the industry of interest to you. You can also add the word directory to other keywords. *The Techra Analyst Firm Directory* is a complete analyst firm directory and *The Tekrati Directory of Analyst Firms* can be found by a keyword search. The Yahoo! Finance website is also worth a look. Here you can enter details of particular companies. Analyst Coverage is listed for each company, containing details of relevant analysts and their firms. Many stock listings will also show analyst details.

Action #2
Look up the websites of several companies within your industry of interest. Company websites usually contain pages listing press releases, articles about the company and/or media coverage. Often articles will refer to or contain quotes from industry analysts and a quick Internet search will usually reveal their contact information.

Company websites also often have a page titled "Investors". Typically, the site will have a statement such as: "We are aware of the following analysts who cover the company", followed by a list of analysts by name and company.

Major consulting and research firms employ analysts. These analysts and their contact information will be listed on their website. For example, the Gartner Group website has profiles of both analysts and consultants.

Action #3

Identify a current industry event, such as a trade show or expo. Log on to the event's website and search for press releases. Analyst articles about the companies attending the event are generally posted there and contact information is often included at the end of articles. If not, the publications in which the articles appear will be and these can be contacted for further information.

Industry or trade publications frequently contain analyst-authored articles. If you don't know the titles of any of these publications, contact the sales department of a company within the industry and ask for details of the publications the sales staff use. Then research these publications online.

PeoplePoints

New Graduates: Analysts can inform you about industry companies that are not in public databases. The key is to ask about high growth companies that would offer entry level positions.

Experienced Professionals: Analysts are a great resource for management level introductions. Given that analysts connect with hundreds of companies a year, adding analysts to your network will be a definite advantage.

Chapter 3: Recruiter Contacts

Why Contact Recruiters?

Contingency and retained recruiters not only find candidates, but they also develop relationships with client industry companies and contacts within those companies. Recruiters are contracted and receive payment from companies. It is important to keep in mind that recruiters work for client companies and not for job candidates. In addition, internal staffing recruiters are company employees and only work to fill positions for their company. Any activity other than filling contracted positions is nonproductive for recruiters.

Recruit a Recruiter

Getting the attention of recruiters in an economic downturn is not as easy as it was a few years ago when recruiters were bountiful and bidding for great candidates. In a candidate-rich market with slow job creation, you need to seek them out. Don't wait to be found.

How can you get a recruiter's attention in this tough job market? The first steps are to:

One: Learn about the types of recruiters.
Two: Research recruiters' specializations.
Three: Understand how recruiters earn their living.

Corporate recruiters can be referred to as in-house staffers and are company employees. They review resumes, and prescreen candidates though company advertisements, job fairs and employee referrals. Prescreened candidates' resumes are delivered to company hiring managers. In difficult job markets, staffing recruiters receive huge volumes of resumes and may limit the number they review to the first fifty or so received.

Retained recruiters are contracted to help fill a specific position and the only recruiters that have the ability to work on that position. Payment to retained recruiters is issued in three stages: one third at the start of the search, another third halfway through the recruitment process and final payment upon completing the placement. Most often they are seeking highly specialized candidates or are recruiting for upper level management positions. Thus companies only hire one recruiting agency for a position.

Contingency recruiters are the most plentiful. They specialize in a specific industry and specific positions. Contingency recruiters contract with multiple companies for multiple jobs. The first contingency recruiter to submit a candidate receives payment for placement if a candidate is hired. Often a candidate is contacted by several recruiters from different agencies for the same position since companies might contract with multiple contingency recruiters.

Retained and contingency recruiters mainly hunt and find candidates through personal referrals, a process that can take many hours of phoning and emailing. Candidates who post their resumes on general job boards are the least likely to be picked up as many recruiters do not even subscribe to these. Some recruiters exclusively use social networks to avoid paying the high fees associated with job board resume databases.

It's best to be selective in how you solicit recruiters. Recruiters only fill from 10% to 15% of jobs. Still, the odds of recruiter placement are better than job board placements, which only fill from 2% to 5% of jobs. If you fulfill the job requirements, work with the recruiter of record to try and secure the position. However, don't waste a recruiter's time if you do not possess the skills and experience needed for the position.

A little bit of extra effort can go a long way. A while back I advertised positions for construction positions at a United States military base in a specific military newspaper. The intention was to focus on a targeted audience. The ad requested resumes be sent by email to PeopleHirePeople®; however, the business phone number was also published.

A prospective job candidate named George called before sending his resume. In conversation George asked for more detail about the company and the job. He asked key questions about the timeframe to fill the position, the history of the company's construction division, the hiring process and additional job requirements that were not detailed in the classified advertisement. I complimented George on the personal contact. George replied, "I can learn more in a five minute phone call than in studying the web for hours."

With this additional firsthand information, George was able to tweak his resume to match his experience to the priority requirements. Taking the time to speak to the recruiter directly and thoroughly research the job requirements enabled George to present his skills and experience more effectively.

It's a good idea to work with recruiters by phone to:

One: Engage in conversation to learn about the additional job requirements.

Two: Tweak your resume to match the exact requirements of the position.

Three: Alert the recruiter that your resume will be arriving.

If a recruiter contacts you first, ask which type of recruiter he or she is. Whether you are employed or unemployed ask for the recruiter's full contact information so you can stay in touch for the future. Offer to assist by referring candidates for positions for which you are not qualified. Nurture the relationship and add recruiters to your career network. Recruiters may prove to be most helpful in the future and can make valuable network connections. But always remember that recruiters are people finders for contracted jobs and not job finders for people needing a job.

How to Hunt Recruiters

Action #1
Use a search engine with a combination of keywords to discover executive recruiting firms. For example, try "executive search firm" plus keywords for the industry of specialization.

Action #2
Explore *The Riley Guide*. It is on the Internet and lists companies in alphabetical order along with the type of firm and area of specialization. You can click on each company's name and link through to its website.

The Directory of Executive & Professional Recruiters, often referred to as the "Red Book", can be purchased or found at libraries. The Directory has been published since 1971 and contains contact information for each company, including names of key contacts, phone numbers, fax numbers, and email and web addresses. The Directory is also available online. Contact your local library or state universities for free access to the online version.

Action #3
To find local recruiters, research your local recruiters' professional associations. States and

cities usually have one or more associations in the area. Many recruiters are boutique firms, which means they are sole proprietors or small firms with just a couple of recruiters. These often don't have a web presence and can only be found through professional associations.

To locate associations in a particular geographic area use keyword searches plus the name of a state. It's best not to use a city name in your search as this will eliminate small cities and suburbs. An example of a good keyword search would be "Missouri recruiters associations".

Alternatively, if you know of a local executive search firm, call them up and find out which professional recruiter associations they belong to. Then contact the associations for details of additional recruiters specializing in your industry of choice and/or type of position you seek.

PeoplePoints

New Graduates: Be sure you understand the functions of the different types of recruiters and staffers. If a recruiter contacts you, ask what type of recruiter he/she is. This will eliminate the potential for confusion and you will know how to enter into the situation.

Experienced Professionals: The most time-effective and productive strategy is to only contact recruiters specializing in the positions and industry relevant to your job hunt. If you are obviously not a good fit for a position, recruiters will not spend time with you as a candidate. When a recruiter contacts you, always respond promptly! If you are not a fit for the position or the position is of no interest to you, offer to assist in candidate referrals. This will help to create a long-term networking connection with the recruiter who will likely reconnect with you if a more appropriate position comes up in the future.

 # How to Hunt

Section B:

How to Hunt

This section tells you how to hunt additional contacts with vast networks. PeopleHirePeople® has identified three groups of key professionals: event contacts, regional contacts and global contacts. Within each group there are three sets of professional contacts.

Network for a Job

Chapter 4: Event Contacts

Event professionals have vast networks comprised of clients, customers and patrons. This group contacts covers professional associations, trade shows and training sessions.

Professional Associations

Seven out of ten people in the United States belong to at least one association and 25% are members of four or more associations. Once you are a member of an association you are invited to attend regular meetings and association events. Such events usually involve informal networking followed by the business agenda and finally a guest speaker or formal presentation.

Once an event has ended members often leave immediately due to other personal or work-related obligations. In this situation it can be difficult to create quality introductions and opportunities for conversation. An alternative tactic is to study the member directory and select key member contacts to target prior to the event. Or you could focus your efforts on the three key contacts that follow and attempt to set up a phone conversation or a one-on-one meeting with them. Note that some associations are for corporations so check for individual memberships.

Association Contacts

Contact #1: Membership Director
Log on to the association website and locate the staff web page. The membership director will have the most up-to-date and comprehensive information about members. The director can indicate members that may be the most appropriate for you to contact according to their position and their company of employment.

Contact #2: Board of Directors
Directors' details, including their titles and company names, can also be found on the association website. Directors are usually very prominent industry professionals.

Contact #3: Committee Chairpersons
Find committees and subcommittees of interest on the association webpage. The chairperson for each committee will be named and their contact information, together with a schedule of committee meetings, may also be available. Committee meetings may provide good

opportunities to make connections in a particular niche or in a smaller, less intimidating venue.

"Real People" Association Connections

Preparing to network at a professional association event is not only essential but easy to do as a member. And if you don't do your homework, you may find yourself losing out on valuable opportunities.

Some time ago, I was invited by a personal friend, the president of the Financial Executives Networking Group (FENG) local chapter, to a special dinner event. The national president of FENG was to be the guest speaker on the topic of job hunting. Consequently, turnout was exceptional as members attended in search of employment.

Discussions during informal networking buzzed around job search. One member, Paul, stated his main target company for employment opportunities was a joint venture company formed by two major defense companies. I asked Paul if he knew the president of the local chapter. Paul replied that this was only his second meeting and he had briefly spoken to him on the phone. I then revealed to Paul that the local chapter president had worked at that company's finance division for more than five years. Paul immediately left the group's presence to seek him out.

The lesson learned was that Paul should have studied the FENG Association's membership directory before the event, particularly as FENG members have full access to data about the entire association's nationwide members through its online directory. Luckily for Paul, he found out through a chance conversation about this valuable networking opportunity, but he could quite easily have left the event without making the connection. In his presentation later that evening, the national FENG president encouraged members to use the directory for job networking and he volunteered to facilitate member-to-member acquaintances.

Ruby, an MBA student from the Krannert School of Management at Purdue University, also realized the value of association networking. Here is an email she wrote to me after instruction in PeopleHirePeople® contact methods:

Dear Ms. Conners,

I was thinking about getting back to you to let you know that I've successfully found a job (within one month) using your method.

I made phone calls to all local chapters of the Product Development Management Association and asked the presidents of those local chapters to tell me leads about companies which were looking for project managers with a product development and MBA background, and also companies that were looking to establish or which had already established business with Asia (particularly China). Most of them were very friendly and helpful and provided me with several leads to follow-on.

I am now working for a niche consulting firm called XXX, which specializes in New Product Development, Innovation Strategy and Product Lifecycle Management consulting serving industry leaders across various industries.

I would like to show my appreciation for the great concept you evangelized and hope you will spread this concept around successfully.

Best regards,
Ruby
Purdue MBA

For Ruby, phone calls proved the fastest method of finding employment possibilities. She took the initiative in contacting all chapters since there was no way for her to attend all the various local chapter meetings. This strategy proved to be time-efficient and results-effective, and Ruby found that most of the individuals she phoned were very receptive and helpful. Their referrals and private firsthand information were key to her new employment.

Hunt Professional Associations

Action #1
Use a search engine and perform a keyword search. The main keyword should reflect the industry of interest and should be followed by the words "association" or "organization". Other useful keywords include "supply chain" or "society".

Action #2
Study the website of one of your target companies to identify the associations to which the company belongs.

Action #3

Research several directories online, such as The ASAE Gateway to Associations Directory, the Directory of Professional and Industry Associations and Societies, and WEDDLE's Association Directory. A business reference librarian at your local public library may also be able to help you track down details.

PeoplePoints

New Graduates: Ask the membership director of the association if there is a student discount for membership or a complementary free membership for new graduates. Before attending a meeting, contact the membership chairperson or director and ask if he or she could arrange for an active member to act as your host for introductions to members at the meeting. This will facilitate ease of introductions.

Experienced Professionals: Always study the directory of members. Make a list of those members with whom you would like to be acquainted. Find out additional information on your target member list via LinkedIn and make notes. When you arrive at the event, check the sign-in registration for those members to see if they are in attendance. Approach members with a nugget of information you have researched about them – perhaps an article they have written or a mutual acquaintance. This common connector will facilitate introductions for you.

Trade Shows

Most job candidates attend trade shows when they are employed and the corporation is picking up the tab. If you're unemployed, however, attending trade shows can be expensive.

A further barrier to making connections is that company representatives are at trade shows to promote and sell their products or services. Their time is fully booked with customers and prospective customers; they cannot afford the time to interview potential future employees. It's best, therefore, to do your research and connect with people associated with trade shows away from the actual event.

Trade Show Contacts

Contact #1: Event Promoter
The individual who works with company representatives who attend trade shows may also be known as the sales manager, corporate relations director or event coordinator. He or

she will have knowledge of new industry companies, companies requiring larger exhibitor space, companies introducing new products or services, or companies with representation on panels and workshops. All of these are potential employment opportunities. The event promoter can refer you to individuals in various companies.

Contact #2: Workshop Panelists and Presenters

Tradeshows offer workshops and super sessions. Flyers for these workshops will list the presenters and panelists, who are usually industry leaders. Often the panel moderators will be industry analysts. Check out the list of workshops, speakers and panelists for great industry connections.

Contact #3: Award Recipients

Check the lists of companies being recognized at industry events. Awards may be given for new products, new services, entrepreneurship or excellent growth. Then find individuals within the companies to contact. A congratulatory greeting will facilitate your introduction. Selection committee members also make great key contacts.

Trade Show Networking

I received an email from the MBA career director of a major Texas university who was seeking assistance for one of his graduating students. The student was looking to get back to Colorado and the career director had lost details of his connections in Denver. The graduating student was targeting a position in customer insights within the pet industry.

With no knowledge of the position, my first step was to learn about the customer insights industry. The Internet was a good starting point for my research. With that initial knowledge I next did a keyword search for major trade shows in the pet industry using the keywords "Colorado customer insights pet industry 2013".

The first result was for a major industry conference, the 2013 Pet Industry's Top2Top Conference. This listed conference attendees along with details of their names, companies and titles. Here were more than seventy-five major industry professionals for the graduate student to contact.

The second search result was for another conference. The details did not include a list of attendees, but more than twenty-five presenters were featured, all professionals within the pet industry. Their bios, their current companies, titles and photos were listed, and presenters included owners, presidents, vice presidents, managers and company founders. Some of these industry people would have connections in Colorado. Again, this was another terrific list with which to begin a pet industry job network.

Anyone can carry out Internet research to discover industry people to connect with. Laser-focus your efforts on networking with real people. Just to remind you, 70 to 85% or more find jobs through networking.

Recruiters, like job candidates, also find the best candidates through networking. There is no difference in the techniques used by job candidates and recruiters. Both have to network to find referrals either to get jobs or to get access to the best candidates for jobs.

As a recruiter, I needed to find a telecommunications candidate in Vancouver, Canada. With absolutely no connections anywhere in Canada and no database, my Internet research using a search engine and keywords led to the Canadian CommTech Show & Seminar, a large tradeshow in Vancouver. I located the director's details on the tradeshow's website and called her. The purpose of our conversation was to learn about the industry, companies and contacts in this location.

I asked the director for permission to email her the job description. After our discussion, she emailed me with an offer to circulate the job description to a couple of her contacts.

A couple of years later and I still receive the show's newsletters via email. The e-newsletters keep us in touch and I also get great up-to-date industry information.

Personal and direct contact builds networks. Establish your relationship and then use email, texting and other digital methods to keep the network alive.

Hunt Trade Shows

Action #1
Use a search engine and perform a keyword search based on a primary word or word that defines the industry followed by the word "tradeshow" or "conference" and the current year. For calendars or lists of tradeshows, use keywords such as "trade shows", "lists" or "tradeshow schedules" along with the current year. To find trade shows in a specific geographic region, research the convention

center in the area. Then call the events manager and ask for a list of trade shows coming to the convention center.

Action #2
Target specific companies and check out one or more company websites. Research web pages labelled "About us" or "Events". These company web pages will have trade show and conference schedules.

Action #3
Contact a salesperson in your industry and ask for details of the best trade shows that the most significant players attend. This is also a great conversation opener in which to learn about the sales professional's database of companies and contacts within those companies.

PeoplePoints

New Graduates: Study the list of exhibitors to learn about industry companies that you may not know. Take particular interest in small to midsize companies as they will create the most jobs. If your job hunt is limited to one specific geographic area, prioritize on those exhibitors with company facilities within your desired location.

Experienced Professionals: Trade shows are costly to attend. Make a list of those you previously attended and network through phone calls. Then research the tradeshow website for previous acquaintances who are staff members, exhibitors, speakers or moderators. If you have no prior connections, start with the event promoter. Compliment him/her about the quality of the event you previously attended. Then ask key questions about companies and contacts within those companies.

Training Sessions

Training sessions can be onsite workshops, certification classes, compliance education, professional seminars, live online training, webinars, tutorials or lecture series. Training sessions that further your career, enable you to obtain certifications or assist with governmental compliance fall into this category. Training industry professionals are great additions to job networks as they have a wealth of industry-specific contacts.

Training Session Contacts

Contact #1: Coordinator

This individual's title could also be engagement director or event manager. This is the person who interacts directly with the professionals signing up for training or managers sending their employees to the session.

Contact #2: Instructors

Instructor profiles can usually be viewed on the training company's website, along with their contact information. Instructors will have information on industry companies, companies sending the attendees and attendees.

Contact #3: Sales

The sales professionals for the training company or the company selling the products offering complementary training will also have current industry information and contacts. Sales professionals use complementary training as a tool to generate additional sales.

Great Networking Opportunity with Training

New graduates may not be aware of the complementary free seminars that feature new products, services or upgrades by vendors. These vendors tend to be Value Added Resellers (VARs).

For example, a new graduate with a mechanical engineering degree may have university experience with only one computer-aided design (CAD) software program. However, real world job experience might require the graduate to have knowledge of another CAD software program. VARS offer complementary free seminars featuring the latest versions of software. Many attendees will be mechanical engineers whose companies already use the product but who would like to either "test drive" the new version, or those who want to learn more about the updated version. Groups of engineers from area companies, plus their managers, are likely to be in attendance.

The graduate should ask permission of the company VAR representative to attend training, explaining how it would assist in job hunting. Time at the beginning and end of the session as well as during breaks present opportunities to network with local mechanical engineers and managers, and this may lead to employment opportunities.

Experienced professionals can also take advantage of connections made in training sessions. Joe was a fifteen year industry IT professional and contacted me after months of unemployment. A quick review of his resume revealed that he did not have a four year degree but that he did hold many certifications and training qualifications.

I asked Joe if he thought he was being rejected by human resources because he lacked a degree. He was sure that this was a factor. However, until now, Joe had also never had to actually search for employment. His current search tactics comprised a review of online applications for advertised jobs. He felt that his years of experience and certifications should at least get him in the door for interviews.

Noting all Joe's certifications and training, I posed the question, "Have you thought about going back to the companies where you acquired your certifications and training for networking?" He had not.

I advised Joe to reconnect with the companies who had provided his training. Asking the event coordinator, salespeople and instructors for details of the companies that were currently sending employees for training would provide Joe with target companies in his desired location. With the names of people within these companies, Joe could engage these new contacts in conversation and obtain referrals to hiring managers. By bypassing human resources and speaking directly to hiring managers, he would be able overcome the lack of a degree.

Nearly 60% of American jobs now require at least a bachelor's degree, according to a 2010 report released by the Center on Education and the Workforce, and this number is expected to grow in the next decade. However, objections to not possessing a bachelor's degree can be overcome through networking.

Hunt Training Sessions

Action #1
Use a search engine and perform a keyword search using a word that reflects the industry followed by words such as "training", "workshop", "certification", "compliance" or "webinar". Remember to add the current year.

Action #2
Contact a human resources manager at one of your target companies and clarify what certifications are required for the position of interest. This is also an opportunity to impress an HR manager and engage in conversation about future openings.

Action #3

Join several industry groups on LinkedIn and pose questions about training sessions. When individual group members make suggestions, take the opportunity to ask them to join your individual network. Then you will have their contact information to call them and discuss training one-on-one. These become great contacts for job connections too.

PeoplePoints

New Graduates: Join LinkedIn industry groups – you are allowed to join up to fifty. On the LinkedIn group discussion page, ask this question: "As a new college graduate, which certifications will I need in the future to keep my skills current and relevant?" After receiving responses from other group members, contact each individually to thank him or her for the advice and obtain permission to invite the person to join your LinkedIn network. Once people have been added to your network, ask for their phone numbers and permission to call them to obtain additional advice. Tell them you appreciate they took the time and effort to respond to your question and that you would like to keep in touch during your job search.

Experienced Professionals: Dig deep to find previous training experiences and take a critical look at your own resume. Did your previous employers send you to training sessions that you haven't listed on your resume? Did you attend seminars at a trade show or conference? Find out who the presenters, moderators and panels were in those sessions and contact them. Are there certifications that you or your potential employees need to possess? With increasing government regulations and legislation across all industries, compliance training sessions offer the opportunity to make great connections.

Chapter 5: Regional Contacts

If you are limited geographically, either because you want to stay in the area you currently reside in or because you wish to relocate to a specific location, you need to think outside the box to uncover jobs. There are three groups of key contacts with networks for specific regions: real estate contacts, professional media contacts and small business contacts.

Real Estate

Real estate professionals can give you an abundance of information about a regional economy and who is creating or losing jobs. If you plan to relocate to another area, it is a good idea to contact several commercial real estate professionals to get a well-rounded view of the area's demographics. Agents work with companies leasing larger spaces, companies relocating to the area and commercial developers, often confidentially. These professionals know what's happening before it is announced in the media.

Real Estate Contacts

Contact #1: Real Estate Agents

Real estate agents represent buyers and sellers, and sometimes act as a dual agency. They are concerned with purchases.

Contact #2: Commercial Leasing Agents

Leasing agents work for the landlords of commercial real estate, including office buildings, industrial parks and mixed-use developments. They find tenants and usually handle all aspects of leases.

Contact #3: Real Estate Property Managers

Property management is the operation, control and oversight of real estate. Property managers can be onsite or on the premises for a specific property or several properties (i.e. an office building). They form a relationship with the property tenants.

Location, Location, Location

Everyone knows that when purchasing either residential or commercial real estate, it's location that achieves best value for your investment. Connections with real estate professionals can be valuable to your job hunt.

Conversations with a couple of top real estate agents are ideal to gather great information whether you are in home territory or relocating somewhere new.

Here are three scenarios that demonstrate how making real estate connections helped in job networking.

Scenario #1

Always make inquiries as I did when I was leasing downtown office space for my recruiting company. Once the lease was signed, I asked the onsite manager about the building's other tenants. My focus was engineering firms, and the leasing manager promptly introduced me to two engineering tenants. Thus I was able to secure placements for engineering candidates into one of the firms. Not only did the leasing onsite manager become a great job source, but the managers in the engineering company have become long-term networking connections who continually make referrals and hires.

Scenario #2

A job candidate walked out of a PeopleHirePeople® seminar and drove to several high-rise office buildings on his way home. He entered the buildings with paper and pencil in hand and headed over to where the building directories were displayed. He was determined to find employment within a ten minute commute from his home.

He copied the names of the companies listed on the building directories and returned home to research them on the Internet. He also planned to ask the leasing agents for introductions into those companies.

Here was a candidate who had taken the "real estate" connection a step further and was doing onsite research for himself!

Scenario #3

The following real estate transaction appeared in the Colorado Springs Real Estate Briefs June 20, 2003 edition of the *Colorado Springs Business Journal* under the subtitle of "Transaction Report".

> <u>Defense Contractor Opens Office</u> from Ted Link at Fidelity Investments, SRA International, a defense contractor expanding into Colorado Springs, leased approximately 6,300 sq. ft. at 4700 East Platte Ave. Link represented the landlord Cavan Investments in the transaction, in collaboration with Julien J. Studley.

If you are limited by location, look in your local news publication for commercial real estate transactions. In the example listing above, two real estate agents could be contacted. Not only could people ask about the particular company referred to in the notice, but this was a door opener to ask the agents about additional companies with whom they were working.

In connection with this specific transaction, I researched the headquarters for SRA International and asked for the phone number of the new facility in Colorado Springs and the new general manager of the facility. Although a phone number for the new facility was not yet available, I was given the name of the general manager and his cell phone number. Our subsequent conversation revealed that he would be hiring about a dozen local individuals and he proceeded to describe the skills that were needed for those new employment opportunities not yet advertised.

Real estate agents possess a lot of regional information, often long before it appears in the local media. If you are restricting your job search to a specific location, be sure to contact several agents to become well-informed and discover more information than you will find on the Internet.

Hunt Real Estate Contacts

Action #1
Drive by key commercial local sites and note the names of realtor agents on building signs and billboards.

Action #2
Use a search engine to find your local real estate association. Good keywords are "local real estate association" plus the name of the city.

Action #3
Contact the Local Association of Realtors. A call to any commercial real estate office should get you the Association's contact information. A directory of real estate associations can also be found on the following website: http://www.realestateassociations.com/.

PeoplePoints

New Graduates: If you are contemplating relocation or a return to your home town, contact several real estate agents in the area. Agents in the same company work on different developments and transactions. Agents can be the easiest people with whom to hone your networking conversation skills.

Experienced Professionals: Call the local board of realtors and ask staff to suggest some top regional sales agents. Speak with top performing agents and those who have been in the industry the longest. These top agents will have a vast amount of current and historical information that will assist your job hunt.

Media

The possibilities that could arise from conversing with media professionals are often overlooked. If a company is featured in the media, job candidates may send a resume or make an online application to that company without stopping to consider the benefits of making a connection with the author of the article. Media professionals have countless connections in order to report, analyze and present information. There is enormous value in tapping their extensive networks.

Media Contacts

Contact #1: Business Reporters

Look for article bylines, which is where you will find the contact information for the reporter/author. Bylines may be directly under the title or at the very end of the article.

Contact #2: Columnists
Browse publications or examine the publication index for details of regular columnists.

Contact #3: Radio Hosts
The radio station's website will list its programs and hosts. Note the production team members too.

Geographic Limits and No Connections

In difficult job markets media reporters spend a significant amount of time featuring job candidates and their inability to secure employment. Reporters then contact career professionals for very specific job search advice for the people they feature.

In April 2011, a *Denver Post* article featured a job candidate having difficulty in his job hunt. He had relocated to the Denver area after losing his job as a restaurant manager at an exclusive golf club in another state. He had had just one face-to-face interview in the past six months. His job search had been limited to online job ads due to a lack of professional contacts in the local area.

The career experts featured in the article advised this job candidate to target his job search by researching companies and contacting the decision makers within those companies. Other suggestions were to go to industry events and join associations to build an industry network.

After careful research, I came up with three major connections for this candidate to pursue.

The first connection could be the business reporter from *The Denver Post* who wrote the article covering the candidate's difficulty in finding employment. This reporter can make introductions to other business reporters who cover the hospitality/restaurant industry. For example, this particular reporter had written an in-depth article on the new CEO for a chain restaurant headquartered in the Denver area. The reporter could have facilitated an introduction to the CEO, potentially leading to further introductions to restaurant managers hiring for positions.

A further possibility is that the reporter, based on his previous research and articles, might be able to provide information about the numerous restaurant or food chains headquartered in the Denver area. My initial research came up with more than fifteen in the Denver geographic area. These chains hire new managers for new facilities, managers to train managers, or managers to work with new franchise owners.

The second major connection is other reporters. There are at least three other regular reporters/columnists for *The Denver Post*. One columnist writes for the business section and often covers new restaurant openings and the players involved. Another columnist pens the home and entertainment column. He wrote a column about university graduates in Denver who are running successful eateries in the area. Yet another columnist in the lifestyle section covers charity, nonprofit and gala events. She knows the major venues for these events and the caterers. Her numerous contacts would comprise major area hotels, country clubs and restaurants.

Reporters and columnists interview key industry professionals in order to obtain firsthand information. Introductions and/or referrals by these key professionals could get a foot in the door for employment. And it's easy to make contact as phone numbers and email addresses are listed for the reporters and columnists in their bylines.

The third major connection is a media contact on the local radio and TV. A well-known Denver talk radio host has been reviewing

Denver area restaurants for more than two decades, and he also has a weekend TV show where he is filmed dining at and reviewing restaurants in the area. What's more, the host in question has obviously referred candidates for restaurant jobs directly to managers and owners as he has asked on-air how his referrals are doing!

These three key connections that could help this candidate into the Denver area restaurant industry came via local media. By speaking directly to these contacts, he could quickly increase his industry referrals and learn about management positions before they are advertised. He would be better placed by taking his job search offline and connecting directly with professionals that have local networks in his industry.

If you are limited geographically in your search for a job, investigate local media for industry clues and contacts. Play detective to uncover those professionals who can assist you with industry connections. Pick up the phone. Ten minutes on the phone will reap industry connections fast.

Hunt Media Contacts

Action #1
Find major newspapers with a search engine and keywords including the name of the city and the word "newspaper".

Action #2
Use a search engine to find business publications. Relevant keywords include the name of the city and the words "Business Journal" or "business publications".

Action #3
Identify local radio programs with an Internet search using keywords including the name of the city and "talk radio" or "radio news". TuneIn Radio is a free Internet service that lists all business programs in all geographic areas. It allows access to thousands of stations and podcasts. Select the business listing on the TuneIn Radio website.

PeoplePoints

New Graduates: Be aware of the many media sources that will help you get the most current information. All media research should result in actually speaking directly with relevant people. You will learn more firsthand information in a ten to fifteen minute conversation than by researching written media for hours.

Experienced Professionals: If you are planning to relocate, subscribe to the region's local newspapers and business publications in print or online versions. Study the information and do not hesitate to call business reporters, columnists and editors to discover more about the area's job market. Note the region's growth companies and contact the salespeople for those companies. Firsthand regional information is important to landing a position in your new location. Make these types of calls and set up interviews before traveling to the area.

Small Business

Seven out of ten jobs are created by small businesses. An effective job hunt includes small business, which is defined by five hundred or less employees. Learn how to interact with professionals in economic development, technology centers and other programs to uncover jobs within small businesses.

Small Business Contacts

Contact #1: Economic Development Staff

Search the website of your local Economic Development Council for the name of the business development officer. There will also be other officers and staffer names. Also check out the Economic Development Department at the state level.

Contact #2: Chamber of Commerce

Call into the organization and ask for the staffer who works with companies in the community. This may be a person in business development, or staffers who serve on other community organizations who are interfacing with local companies.

Contact #3: Technology Contacts

The Federal Laboratory Consortium for Technology Transfer (FLC) has complete contact information listed on its website for regional contacts, executive boards, national advisors, committee chairs and agency representatives. Select a few with whom to phone and converse.

The *National Business Incubation Association*'s website lists executives, board of director members and other staffers. Select several and contact them. The website also lists the United

States State Incubation Associations together with details of the directors or chairpersons and their contact information.

Hunt Where Others Don't

Super creative research is required for a geographically limited job hunt. Small businesses are frequently overlooked by job candidates because they often do not advertise jobs. However, small businesses create the most jobs. Candidates who compile the best database of local small companies and contacts within those companies will increase employment opportunities. Stop competing for the same few advertised jobs with the same few large corporations, and hunt small businesses.

If you find you are technologically challenged in researching local small businesses or simply want to cut your research time to a minimum, book a private session with a business librarian at your local public library. A good business librarian will be efficient in online search techniques and will retrieve information easily. Librarians can show you databases you may not be able to find online yourself. Businesses librarians are great hidden hunting tools!

When faced with the task of job development for a Fortune 100 company shutting a large manufacturing facility, one of the first professionals I called was the VP of Business and Industry for the local Chamber of Commerce. The VP graciously agreed to meet. His focus was local economic development, manufacturing, small business, and business retention and expansion programs.

Not only did I meet with the VP, but he invited me to meetings of the local manufacturing association. I had the opportunity to meet many manufacturing managers and owners, and these introductions resulted in employment for many individuals caught up in the layoff. Years later, I can pick up the phone and catch-up with the now former VP of the local Chamber of Commerce. Quality networking means great lifelong connections.

A software developer candidate, Steve, living in a small mountain town with a population of less than five thousand, hoped to avoid an hour long commute to the closest major city. Steve wrote to me to relate how he was hired for an unadvertised job after learning PeopleHirePeople® job hunting methods.

I went to the Chamber of Commerce to see if there were any software companies in Woodland

Park. They knew of two that were bigger than a single person. I was able to look one of them up on the Internet. The company, ConfigureSoft, makes a great tool for keeping track of PC configurations (things like installed hardware, disk space, software versions, etc.). I thought this would also be useful for Linux and other UNIX systems, so I went to the company and asked for the name of the Marketing Manager. I was hoping to send a letter suggesting that I help them port their software. Luckily, the VP of Product Development overheard and it resulted in an interview that afternoon! They already had customers requesting the Linux port. Talk about accidental timing! If I hadn't gone to the Chamber, I still wouldn't know that ConfigureSoft existed!

Thanks again!!

Steve

Local business alliances are similar to chambers of commerce and can also make great regional connections. Their goal is to attract investment into an area, either through relocation or company expansion. Keep an eye on local media for alliance briefing reporters, or better still, get in direct contact.

Another creative research area for small businesses is centers for technology. Daily lives have been changed due to technology. You can find employment with a high-tech company without being high-tech yourself – these companies still need marketing, administration and sales staff.

Hunt Small Business Contacts

Action #1

Research economic development directories. A good directory website is the *Economic Development Directory* (http://www.ecodevdirectory.com).

This site lists economic development agencies in the United States by individual states, as well as agencies in other countries. Another useful website is the Site Selection Web (http://www.sitenet.com/portal/index.shtml), which includes a guide to private and governmental economic development agencies. This site provides complete contact information on the professionals in each agency and their individual websites.

Action #2

Find the local Chamber of Commerce. A keyword search in a search engine will easily find the regional economic agency and the Chamber of Commerce in your region.

Action #3

Identify local technology centers. An Internet keyword search will find incubator, entrepreneurial and technology centers. Useful keywords are the name of the city of preference and words such as "incubator center", "entrepreneurs" or "technology center". Also try the name of a state or keywords "technology council".

Contact your local universities as many of these house or sponsor incubator or entrepreneurial centers. Or contact The Federal Laboratory Consortium for Technology Transfer (FLC), which is the nationwide network of federal laboratories. The FLC is a forum to develop strategies and opportunities for linking laboratory mission technologies and expertise with the marketplace. Member laboratories are listed by regions and states. You could also get in touch with the National Business Incubation Association (NBIA), which is the world's leading organization advancing business incubation and entrepreneurship for companies. The NBIA serves over nineteen-hundred members in sixty-plus countries.

PeoplePoints

New Graduates: Impress small business owners and managers by taking the initiative to pick up the phone and call them. New graduates generally use digital means as the primary form of communication. Demonstrate your difference and use your human voice.

Experienced Professionals: If you perceive you may have been discriminated against when not selected for positions in the past, focus on small businesses. Small business presidents and owners will welcome your wealth and years of experience. Experienced professionals can assist small businesses to get to the next level. Find small businesses that will appreciate your valued expertise.

Chapter 6: Global Contacts

This chapter demonstrates where to hunt for global employment connections. The search starts with international consulates. Consulates are similar to diplomatic offices but focus on dealing with individual persons and businesses. Many countries maintain several consulates in a number of United States cities. Trade agencies and organizations with international affiliations are also useful global contacts.

International Consulates

Embassies and consulates are found in cities worldwide, and diplomatic offices are needed to facilitate international relationships. Consulates perform duties such as issuing passports and verifying citizenship, facilitating business issues and mediating with local officials in cases involving legal matters or other diplomatic matters.

Consulate Contacts

Contact #1: Business Affairs Office

Identify the individual or individuals within the consulate associated with the business affairs office and connect with them. This could be the business development officer.

Contact #2: Consul General

This is the person in charge of a consulate, and he or she may also be known as a consulate-general. The person's name and contact information is usually on the consulate website.

Contact #3: Staffers within the consulates

These individuals' details will also be found on the consulate website. Call and ask for the business affairs office and inquire as to the person who would be most helpful to visit within the office.

Go Global: Start with Consulates

Working for an international company is a dream for many candidates, particularly for those proficient in foreign languages. The trouble is many do not have any contacts. So where do you start if you have zero international connections? Try a consulate.

Strangely enough, local newspapers can be a great place to start a global hunt. A newspaper headline in *The Denver Post* of February 3, 2012 sparked my interest. The article was about the British Consul General residing in Denver, Colorado.

This article revealed that the British Consul General works with Colorado companies that want to expand into the United Kingdom. She was also assigned to assist British citizens with passports and legal issues as well as also working with Britain-based academic institutions on their research projects in the United States.

Further investigation on the British Embassy website reveals that nine United States cities host British consulates.

To find either foreign companies with business interests in the United States or United States companies interested in doing business abroad, start with consulate personnel. An Internet search using the keywords "Denver Consulates", for example, reveals over fifteen other consulates hosted by the City of Denver.

Begin an international job hunt with contacts in consulates. Learn firsthand information about employment possibilities from consulate representatives.

Hunt Consulate Contacts

Action #1
A keyword search using the words "international consulates in the United States" brings up various websites, including the websites of international embassies in the United States.

Action #2
Research directories. Details of foreign consular offices in the United States can be found on the United States Department of States' website (http://www.state.gov/s/cpr/rls/fco). Another directory can be found on the Go Abroad website (http://embassy.goabroad.com/embassies-in/united-states).

Action #3
Find local consulates. Visit the websites of your local state and locate the Governor's Office webpage for a listing of consulates in your area.

PeoplePoints

New Graduates: Consulates offer programs for new graduates. For example, the Japanese government sponsors the Japan Exchange and Teaching (JET) Program. This program invites college graduates to experience living and working in Japan. Its goals are to improve foreign language education and promote international exchange.

Experienced Professionals: Consulates are good additions to job hunt networks for candidates with previous extensive overseas travels, previous employment with extensive ties to a particular country, or those who have been expatriates or are multilingual.

Trade Agencies

Trade agencies bring together resources to assist businesses in today's global marketplace. These agencies offer export assistance and service programs, financial and free trade guides, public-private partnerships information and market research.

Trade Agency Contacts

Contact #1: International Trade Administration (ITA at trade.gov)
The ITA lists over twenty-five senior staffers along with their individual biographies on its website.

Contact #2: Export.gov
This website lists the United States trade agency offices for over one hundred cities. Specific contacts can be found on the website of each city office.

Contact #3: Company Awards
Ask senior staffers about those United States companies that have won the President's "E" Award. The President's "E" Award was created by the Executive Order of the President in 1961 to recognize people, firms or organizations that significantly contribute to the effort to increase United States exports. See http://trade.gov/cs/eaward.asp.

Know Where to Hunt

Most job candidates search for a position and then try to fit their skills and experience into the position. This was Frank's situation when he contacted me. Frank had also worked for a single company for so long that he did not have many professional contacts outside of that company.

With four university degrees and more than fifteen years of work experience, the past ten with a Fortune 100 company, Frank found himself in a reduction of force situation. He was frustrated at not having found a job within a month of his layoff. I listened to Frank's ten minute dissertation about how his skills fit into a particular job I was working to fill. With his justifications and rationalization, he could not grasp that he would not be a good candidate for this particular position.

I explained to Frank, "It is as if you are taking your size 12 foot and trying to make it fit into a shoe that is size 10." Frank chuckled. Like most job candidates, he was determined to demonstrate his eligibility for any advertised job he could find, citing the transferability of his skills. Out of sheer frustration, Frank was spending too much time trying to convince himself and recruiters that he qualified for each and every advertised position. He was so busy competing for the same few advertised jobs that he was spending no time on networking.

I posed the question: "What sets you apart from other job candidates who have your same basic skills and experience?" Frank did not know.

I found two distinguishing factors. Frank was fluent in Spanish, but this skill was listed at the very bottom of his resume in smaller type. His English was flawless without a trace of an accent. To reveal the second, I asked, "Did you travel in your positions?" It turned out he had travelled extensively for work, mainly internationally, but his resume made no mention of this fact.

Fluent Spanish and frequent international travel were clues that Frank should be seeking an international job. Frank's job hunt needed to focus on US companies doing business in Latin American and South American countries or vice versa. His best starting point for making great networking contacts was trade agencies.

State agencies compile directories and lists for foreign trade offices, lists of trade events, foreign sister city programs, export statistics, international consultants, export financing, foreign investments, trade centers and trade zones. Professionals within these foreign trade offices are listed on their websites.

There are infinite possibilities when it comes to international job hunting. The most important factor to remember when researching trade agencies is to visit directly with key agency staff members. These staff members can give updated information not found on agency websites as well as direct personal referrals.

Hunt Trade Agency Contacts

Action #1
Use a search engine. Try keyword searches beginning with the city name then followed by a combination of these words: "export", "international trade", "economic development" or "commerce".

Action #2
Contact the U.S. & Foreign Commercial Service. This is the trade promotion arm of the United States Department of Commerce's International Trade Administration. You can log onto this website and find commercial service trade professionals in more than one hundred United States cities. The United States Commercial Service helps United States companies get started in exporting or increase sales to new global markets in more than seventy-five countries.

Action #3

Explore the Export.gov website. This website has a wide range of current industry and trade information to help exporters of United States goods and services find the information they need to compete successfully in overseas markets. There are success stories, trade events and international offices website.

PeoplePoints

New Graduates: Focus on trade agencies if you majored in a foreign language and need to start a network with ties to a particular country or countries for your language major.

Experienced Professionals: If you have been employed overseas or traveled extensively abroad in your career but lost connections, make new contacts in the various trade organizations.

International Affiliated Organizations

International affiliated organizations create memberships with a global/international scope and presence. Common connectors facilitate and generate the organization's activities.

International Organization Contacts

Contact #1: Organizations

The membership manager or membership chairperson within the organization is a good person to first contact. This membership manager commutes directly with individual members and can supply first hand private information due to their connections.

Contact #2: Organizations

Contact board members, staff and chairpersons for various committees in specific organizations. Most will be listed on their individual websites.

Contact #3: The Federation of International Trade Associations (FITA)

FITA has a membership directory on its website (go to http://fita.org/members_dir.html). Find an organization of interest and visit its website. Contact key personnel within that organization.

Find Common Connectors

If you face major limitations or challenges in your search for employment, you need to connect with others who have faced the same set of challenges in the past. These individuals may be able to assist you with factors such as country of origin, language, work permits or visas as well as entering specific into industries or positions.

I had been contracted to work with MBA students for one-on-one consultations. In particular, I consulted with MBA graduate foreign students who were having difficulty finding potential employment. The difficulty these students were experiencing was that they needed H-1B work authorization. The H-1B work authorization is strictly limited to employment by sponsoring employers. Consequently, these students had to narrow their job search to companies that would consider sponsorship. Many employers will not participate in hiring and sponsoring foreigners for employment.

I suggested that these students find individuals who had, in their previous employment, faced the same barrier of requiring a work visa for the United States. For several students whose nationality was Chinese and who possessed undergraduate degrees in engineering, I performed several keyword searches using different combinations of "Chinese, Asian, American, United States, Engineering, Association and Organization". The search results revealed several organizations for the students to contact.

Three organizations seemed to be particularly relevant. The Silicon Valley Chinese Engineers Association (SCEA) is a non-profit professional organization founded in 1989. Its mission is to promote collaboration, professionalism and entrepreneurship among SCEA members and to serve as well as to protect the members' professional and business interests. SCEA is one of the biggest Chinese professional organizations in the United States with 6,646 members.

The Chinese-American Engineers and Scientists Association of Southern California (CESASC) is a non-profit organization dedicated to promoting the interests, aspirations and professional excellence of Chinese-American engineers and scientists. CESASC provides career and educational advancement opportunities, technical exchange, fellowship and community service. The Chinese Institute of Engineers USA (CIE-USA) is a non-profit professional organization of Chinese-American engineers, scientists and other professionals and was founded in 1917. The objectives of CIE-USA are to promote Science, Engineering, Technology and Mathematics (STEM) in all communities across the United States and provide recognition to APA professionals at the national level.

I recommended that the students contact the executive team, board members, committee chairpersons and volunteers in these three organizations. It would be possible to pose questions of these organizations to find out which members had experience of getting their first United States job with a work visa requirement. Members would be able to relate their personal experience and provide insights into companies that would participate in visa sponsorship. Their common connectors of ethnicity, heritage and industry would make it easy to connect with these professionals.

Identify the common connectors that you can use to research new professional contacts and engage them in conversation. This applies to all new professional networking contacts and is not limited to sharing a language or culture.

Hunt International Organizations

Action #1
Carry out a keyword search. Use a word that relates to a particular nationality or ethnicity, such as the name of a country, along with keywords such as "American" or "United

States" and "organization" or "association". For example: "Chinese American Engineers".

Action #2

Investigate three directories. Check with the local public library or public university's library for relevant directories. The American Chambers of Commerce Abroad (AmChams) advances the interests of American business overseas. It is a voluntary association of American companies and individuals doing business in a particular country, as well as firms and individuals of that country who operate in the United States. Currently, 115 AmChams in 102 countries are affiliated with the United States Chamber of Commerce.

The World Chamber of Commerce Directory lists up-to-date reliable contact information for United States chambers of commerce, economic development councils (EDCs), United States embassies, convention and visitor bureaus (CVBs), Canadian chambers and much more. With over 10,000 listings, the data you need is at your fingertips.

The Chamber of Commerce Directory (www.worldchamberdirectoryonline.com/) lists United States chambers of commerce, Canadian chambers of commerce, EDCs, CVBs, state tourism boards, foreign chambers abroad and located in the United States and foreign embassies in the United States. The directory can be purchased for a nominal fee in .pdf format.

Action #3

Get in touch with The Federation of International Trade Associations (FITA). The Association has 450 members and 450,000 linked company members dedicated to the promotion of international trade, import-export, international logistics management and international finance. This website has comprehensive listings of over 200 agencies with international affiliations.

PeoplePoints

New Graduates: Some organizations with international affiliations, such as The Association of Women in International Trade (www.wiit.org), have discounted membership rates for full-time students. Just before you graduate join major organizations for networking benefits and the organization's newsletters. Other international organizations are listed on the website: http://en.wikipedia.org/wiki/List_of_international_professional_associations.

Experienced Professionals: Private companies such as Selling Simplified (www.sellingsimplified) help businesses expand into foreign markets. These companies will have global offices in various locations worldwide. Companies will also have career webpages for job hunting opportunities.

 What to Ask

Section C:
What to Ask

Ask key questions to facilitate networking conversations. Ask the right questions of the right people and they will share firsthand private information that is so essential to successful job hunts. Asking questions will reap referrals and referrals may lead you to direct connections with hiring managers.

This section provides key, referral and permission questions for specific professionals. Sample networking PeopleScripts are provided. Gracious networking etiquette in communications, specifically email, thank you notes, tracking contacts and follow-up contact with professionals in your new job network, are provided.

Chapter 7: Questions

This chapter lists three key questions you can ask the professionals identified in Sections A and B. These initial key questions facilitate networking and should be casually integrated into conversations. Permission questions are essential to demonstrate respect and facilitate introductions. Lastly, incentive questions can assist you in navigating through company contacts to gain access to hiring managers.

Key Questions

In meaningful conversation, key questions take the focus from you, the job candidate, and move it on to the person you are engaging with. This eliminates the need for you to make a potentially awkward "elevator speech" or launch an equally awkward "sell yourself" campaign. Using key questions in conversation demonstrates your insightfulness and intuition. Focus demonstrates your interest in the other party. Asking questions also requires you to be a great listener, enabling your new professional contact to share their personal firsthand information and knowledge.

The following questions provide the opportunity to gain industry and company referrals.

Questions for Sales Professionals

What companies would you consider your best repeat customers?

What firms are your major industry competitors?

What are the best conferences and tradeshows held by the industry?

Questions for Industry Analysts

What companies are new to the industry?

Which companies are introducing new industry products/services this year?

Are you speaking or moderating at any conferences or seminars?

Questions for Contingency Recruiters

What is your industry and positions for placement?

Do you work directly with hiring managers and how do your review candidates with him/her?

How long have you been placing professionals in this industry?

Questions for Professionals with Associations

Which member companies are experiencing growth?
Which members would be most receptive to visiting with me about the industry?
Which companies not currently members would the association like as members?

Questions for Professionals with Trade Shows

What companies are new to the show?
Which attending companies are leasing more booth space this year?
Which industry analysts will be presenters or moderators at show sessions?

Questions for Professionals with Training Sessions

What companies continually send employees for training/certifications?
Which are new companies sending employees for training/certifications?
Do you offer complementary sessions? If so, would it be possible for me to attend?"

Questions for Real Estate Professionals

Which new companies moving into the region have not received media attention?
Which companies are looking at leasing larger space?
Can you tell me about companies engaging in building or buying new facilities?

Questions for Media/Reporters

Do you have articles/press releases not yet published featuring companies of interest?
Have you recently interviewed any industry leaders?
Can you recommend some industry publications I should subscribe to?

Questions for Professionals with Technology Centers

Can you tell me about the companies currently in the facility?
Is there information on those successful companies that have left the technology center?
Can you tell me which organizations/associations work with the center assisting companies?

Questions for Professionals with Foreign Consulates

What US companies have contacted the consulate about doing business with your country?

Do you have businesses from your country looking for United States liaisons here?

What culture/business events will you sponsor that will be open to professionals from the United States?

Questions for Professionals with Trade Agencies

Does the agency print a list of United States companies that currently trade with specific countries?

What companies have made the most recent inquiries?

What type of seminars or conferences will your agency be hosting this year?

Questions for Professionals with International Affiliated Organizations

Does your organization compile a list of companies and contacts within those companies?

Which committee chairpersons would be receptive to speak with me?

Would it be possible to receive your organization's e-newsletter?

PeoplePoints

New Graduates: You can interchange questions depending on which professionals you speak to. Questions get a network contact in "thinking mode" and make it easier for them to think of industry connections and referrals within specific companies. This is the job networking process.

Experienced Professionals: A short phone conversation is often better for networking purposes because many of the very experienced professionals you will contact do not have time for a lunch or coffee date due to their schedule or travel. By asking for a "date" you put them in the position of saying no. Better to ask them for a few moments on the phone where they will agree to do it immediately or confirm another time for a quick conversation.

Referral Questions

Referrals are great door openers. Great networkers get great referrals. You definitely want to ask for referrals.

What to Ask When Professionals Refer Specific Companies

"Do you have a referral within the companies you suggested?"

Ask this question to prompt the professional for details of specific referrals/employees within each company. Referrals are the best entry into any company as these will help you obtain firsthand knowledge of employment opportunities and make direct connections with hiring managers. Make the call if you are given a referral. If your contact volunteers to make an introduction to the referral, he or she will make the call for you. Either way, you will have established a direct connection.

What to Ask When a Referral Name in a Specific Company Has Been Given

"Can you please give me the correct spelling of the referral's name?"

You need the correct spelling so you can research the referral's details on LinkedIn or via an Internet search. Having some insight into the person's experience and background helps you to connect successfully. You will be better prepared for the networking opportunity.

What to Ask When Professionals Give a Specific Referral's Name

"Would it be appropriate for me to directly contact your referral or would you prefer to make the introduction?"

Self-evaluate your rapport with your contact to know whether or not it's appropriate to ask this professional to make the introduction.

PeoplePoints

New Graduates: Note taking is essential throughout the networking process. You will gain a great deal of information and insight, and you will only retain this detail if you take good notes. You will need accurate notes to help with referral names and permission questions in the next section.

Experienced Professionals: It's best to keep track of your notes by using contact management software. This allows for an easy tracking system and retrieval system with referrals.

Permission Questions

What to Ask When Given a Referral

Graciously thank the contact for the referral and then ask:

"May I use your name when I contact the referral you gave me?"

Asking for permission to use the professional's name demonstrates respect and your new networking professional will hold you in high esteem. The goodwill generated from asking this permission question will be tenfold. This professional will be more likely to refer you in the future.

Using the professional's name when contacting the referral is a major door opener and establishes commonality in the new relationship.

What to Ask When Closing All Conversations with Networking Contacts

"May I invite you to connect on LinkedIn?"

Always close the conversation by asking for permission to connect on LinkedIn. LinkedIn enables you to stay connected and view this contact's career changes. It also keeps the relationship on a business level.

An alternative closing question is:

"May I have your email address so I can keep in touch with you?"

Ask for the contact's work or personal email address if you feel comfortable doing so.

What to Ask if the Contact Has Been Extremely Helpful and You Are Comfortable Enough to Ask

"May I send you a copy of my resume?"

Ask this and the previous questions if you have succeeding in building a good rapport and connection with the new contact. Offer to send your resume, especially if the contact requests a copy, in case other connections come to mind in the future. If you do not feel comfortable asking this question, your email signature should include a link to your resume (refer to the email Thank You Notes section of this guide for an example).

PeoplePoints

New Graduates: Always be respectful of people's time and efforts in assisting you to make connections. Make it a point to thank them during the conversation. When they give you permission to connect on LinkedIn, be sure to email a specific thank you note for this new connection after he or she has accepted your request.

Experienced Professionals: Adding your new referrals to your connections on LinkedIn will allow you to study their connections for additional industry or geographical contacts.

Chapter 8: Conversations

You have carefully performed online research and identified professionals with whom you would like to connect. This chapter shows you how to put it all together to achieve great networking conversations. Using the three elements of job networking conversation, you will learn how to converse specifically for a job. Key referral and permission questions are incorporated into conversations. Actual spoken conversation, whether it is in person or on the phone, allows you to project your personality and create a positive impression.

PeopleScripts for networking with sales professionals, industry analysts and recruiters are included in this chapter, along with effective voicemail PeopleScripts if you cannot speak directly to the person.

Three Elements of a Job Networking Conversation

Conversation Element #1: Opening

Your introductory greeting should include an explanation as to how you have come to make the connection - the "common connector". This turns any conversation or phone call from cold to warm, and you eliminate the need for the person to be curious as to why you have contacted them. You also create an opportunity to make a positive good impression by elaborating on how you have come to initiate the connection. This explanation creates a positive environment within which to proceed. It never hurts to throw in a compliment too.

PeopleScript Starters with "Common Connectors"

"The commentary you wrote for this association's newsletter was a real eye opener and I wanted to seek you out at this meeting."

"I was referred to you by Bill Smith who highly recommended you and suggested I give you a call."

"The discussion you led on LinkedIn was very interesting and I felt the need to speak with you directly."

"I see you were a guest speaker at the latest XXX Expo. Unfortunately, I was unable to attend, but I wanted to visit with you directly."

"Your article titled "How Companies Introduce New Products Successfully", which appeared in the industry trade publication this month, peaked my interest to contact you."

"I noticed you graduated from XX University, as I did."

Conversation Element #2: Content with Questions

Facilitate the conversation with appropriate questions. Questions allow your contact to respond with relevant information that will assist you in your job hunt. Ask a question (some examples of key questions were given a little earlier), and then pause. Be sure to allow time for your contact to respond to each question. Take careful notes of their responses.

Conversation Element #3: Closing

Be gracious and thank the contact for their time, information, advice and referrals. Make sure you address your final thanks using the name of your network contact. Again, a compliment in closing never hurts!

PeopleScript Closers with Thanks

"John, I am most appreciative that you spent the time to give me such wonderful industry insight."

"Jane, thank you for taking time from your busy schedule today to visit with me."

"Bob, I look forward to keeping in touch with you and thank you for allowing me to spend time with you at this event."

"Tom, visiting with you was so inspirational for my job search. I can't wait to put to use all the great information you shared with me. Thanks so much again."

"Joan, you are an exceptional professional in the industry and I am so grateful for all your terrific advice. It meant so much to me to be able to speak with you directly. Thanks again."

PeopleScripts

PeopleScript: Professional Sales

You: Hello John, this is [your full name]. How are you today?
Sales professional: Fine, thank you.

You: Do you have a couple of minutes to visit with me as I would like to tap into your expertise?

Sales professional: What is this concerning?

You: I have a new challenge ahead of me and I am interested in gathering some firsthand information about the industry and companies.

Sales professional: What is it you are needing to know?

You: My personal challenge is to find new employment. I am going about it differently than just applying online. Your assistance with firsthand knowledge and industry expertise could assist me in streamlining my job search. Do you have a couple of minutes for a few questions?

Sales professional: Sure.

You: Can you tell me which companies in the area are experiencing growth?

Sales professional: I can think of a few companies I call on. What type of position are you looking for?

You: A marketing position.

Sales professional: [Elaborates on a few companies].

You: I really appreciate the information. Would you happen to have a contact in the companies that I could call?

Sales professional: Call John Smith in ABC and Jane Smith in XYZ.

You: Do I have your permission to mention your name when I call them?

Sales professional: Sure.

You: Have you attended any recent industry tradeshows that I could study online?

Sales professional: You might take a look at the XXX Expo. It is probably the best in the industry.

You: Thanks, I will definitely research them. I appreciate all the great information you have shared with me this afternoon and I will follow through on the referrals you gave me.

Sales professional: Glad to do it.

You: Would it be possible for me to keep you informed as to my job search? You have been so helpful with firsthand information and great advice I could have never found on the Internet. And if I uncover a new industry startup that might be of interest to you, I will pass it on to you.

Sales professional: Sure.

You: Thanks again and I am looking forward to staying in touch with you.

PeopleScript: Industry Analyst

You: Hello John, this is [your full name]. I read that you were a moderator at the last XYZ conference in Atlanta. Do you have a few minutes to talk?

Industry analyst: Sure. What can I do for you?

You: As an analyst you are engaged with so many industry companies and it would be a privilege for me to tap into your knowledge about some of those companies. I think your expertise and firsthand information will be of great assistance in helping me focus my efforts in my job search. Can I ask you a couple of quick questions?

Industry analyst: Yes.

You: Let me first preface this with an appreciation for your time. I know that you must have a demanding schedule. My goal is to find a few select companies that have high growth in today's market. Could you please tell me which companies you cover might fit into this category?

Industry analyst: [Responds with names of several companies].

You: Is there anyone specific within these companies whom you recommend I contact?

Industry analyst: Mr. Right in ABC Company and Ms. Left in XYZ Company.

You: May I use your name when contacting these people?

Industry analyst: I prefer that you do not use my name.

You: I will respect your confidentiality and not use your name when contacting these referrals.

Can you tell me which industry trade publications I should be reading?

Industry analyst: My recommendations would be ABC magazine and XYZ Quarterly.

You: Would you recommend another analyst who might be an interesting person to contact who covers a crossover industry and would be open to visiting with me?

Industry analyst: Contact Bill Smith at JKL Company. He is a buddy of mine.

You: I can't thank you enough for the referral, the generous amount of information you've given and all the time you have taken with me on the phone today.

Industry analyst: My pleasure and good luck.

You: One last thing, could I send you an invite on LinkedIn?

Industry analyst: Sure.

You: Thanks again for everything. I will catch up with you on LinkedIn.

PeopleScript: Contingency Recruiter

You: Hello this is [your full name] and I would like to speak with one of your senior recruiters about xxx positions.

Recruiting firm: Let me put you in touch with John Smith.

You: Thank you.

Recruiter: Hello this is John Smith. How can I assist you?

You: I am searching for xxx position and was wondering if I might fit into any of the current jobs you are filling.

Recruiter: We have several in that industry. Tell me about your skill set.

You: [Explanation of skills and previous positions.]

Recruiter: Yes, we have a xxx position with a local company. [He proceeds to tell you about the position.]

You: That sounds like a position for which I have the right qualifications. I would like to ask you a couple of additional questions pertaining to this position. Can you tell me if you are working directly with the hiring manager?

Recruiter: Yes, I am. Why do you ask?

You: I find that recruiters who work directly with hiring managers have a better understanding of what a hiring manager really needs besides a skill set, such as personality fit, work ethics and expectations of the candidate.

Recruiter: Interesting.

You: Can you give me the company website so I can evaluate whether it is a company to which I would give you permission to present my resume?

Recruiter: No.

You: I prefer to know the company so that I can study their website in order to better prepare my resume. However, if you cannot, would you email me the exact job description so that I can make sure my resume contains experience pertaining to the requirements?

Recruiter: Yes.

You: After receiving the complete job description, I will return an email with my updated resume. One more thing: if ever I can assist you with job candidate referrals for positions in the industry, please do not hesitate to contact me for referrals. I might have someone in my network that could fit your other positions.

Recruiter: That would be great so I will also send you other job descriptions.

You: I will see what I can do. Also, I am doing a fairly aggressive job campaign and when I uncover some companies with unadvertised jobs to which I don't qualify, I will email you that information. Thanks for your time and I look forward to working with you in the near future.

PeoplePoints

New Graduates: Incorporating phone calls into your job networking strategy makes your effort more productive and cost-effective and will quickly generate additional referrals for you.

Experienced Professionals: As an experienced professional do your homework on the background of your new contact. You might have something in common on experience that you should incorporate into the conversation with additional questions pertaining to the shared experience.

Voicemail

Start a greeting using the contact's name. Your full name should be immediately followed by your cell phone number. Then leave a brief message, which includes the reason why you are calling. This can be conveyed by naming the person who made the referral (if you have his or her permission to do so) or the "common connector" between you and the contact.

End the voicemail by repeating your full name and your cell number. Make sure you speak slowly when stating these so that the message recipient can easily write both down without replaying the voicemail a second or third time.

If the recipient has forwarded his or her phone to another phone then caller ID will not be activated. In this circumstance, state your cell phone number twice in the voicemail. Some phones will not have caller identification technology. Also, the recipient might be accessing voice messages from another phone so again viewing caller ID won't be possible.

PeopleScript Voicemail #1

John, this is [your full name] at xxx-xxx-xxxx. John Smith referred me to you. At your convenience, would you please return my call? I would like to visit with you about some industry information that will be of assistance to a search I am conducting. Thank you. [Your full name] at xxx-xxx-xxxx. (cell number).

PeopleScript Voicemail #2

John, this is [your full name) at xxx-xxx-xxxx. I would appreciate a return call as I would like to tap into your industry expertise for a new endeavor of mine. Please call me at your convenience. I promise it will be a brief conversation. My number is xxx-xxx-xxxx (cell number) and again this is [your full name].

PeopleScript Voicemail #3

John, this is [your full name] at xxx-xxx-xxxx (cell number). My call concerns the recent article that appeared in the ABC association's newsletter and I would appreciate additional information concerning this. Thank you, [your full name] xxx-xxx-xxxx.

PeoplePoints

New Graduates: For all business voice messaging start with your name then state your cell phone number and end the message by repeating both your name and cell phone number. You can also leave your email address if it is a simple address. If you do this, it is good job hunting practice and business etiquette to have an email address that incorporates your name.

Experienced Professionals: For job hunting, only use your cell number. One number for email, voice mail, resumes etc. gives the most professional impression. You have complete control of the communication device without involving others, which reduces the risk of you missing any messages in your job hunt.

Chapter 9: Follow-Up

Follow-up is imperative in the networking process. Be aware of the positive impression this leaves with all those you encounter.

Writing thank you notes, tracking new contacts and staying connected will help you develop your new professional and business network for life. Consequently, if you need another job in the future, you can call on an already established network. The most successful professionals follow up when they say they will! Following up on your initial contact demonstrates good manners and is best business practice.

Thank You Emails

Brief thank you notes are a vital part of job networking and will set you apart from the competition. Usually, job candidates wait until the interviewing process to start penning thank you notes but you should begin the practice in the networking stage of your job hunt.

All the professionals who have assisted you in your networking need to be thanked! Essentially, you are thanking them for sharing their time and information with you. Acknowledge how grateful you are that they shared their time, information, connections, referrals and introductions. Reiterate your "common connector" in the thank you note.

Thank you notes reinforce name recognition and raise your profile, and these should become routine practice in your networking. Being gracious elevates you in the mind of your new networking contacts and facilitates a long-term connection. Emailed thank you notes are often favorable because you can send these quickly and efficiently.

Sample Thank You Emails

Thank You Email #1

Subject: A Brief Note of Thanks

John,

You are most knowledgeable about the industry and I am grateful you shared firsthand information with me. All of it will be most valuable in my job hunt. I am fortunate Bob Smith referred you to me.

Thank you for taking time in your busy schedule to visit with me and I look forward to connecting with you on LinkedIn.

Regards,

Full Name: First and Last
Cell Phone Number and City of Current Residence, State
Email Address
Link to Resume Webpage or Resume Document
Linked in Profile Connection

Thank You Email #2

Subject: Connecting at ABC Association

Jack,

It was great to meet you at the ABC Association last evening. Thank you for sharing your personal experiences with the association. Your industry expertise and knowledge provided me with great insight and will be most helpful in my job hunt. I am most appreciative of the time you took for our one-on-one conversation and I have made numerous notes that will be beneficial in my search.

Thanks,

Full Name: First and Last
Cell Phone Number and City of Current Residence, State
Email Address
Link to Resume Webpage or Resume Document
Linked in Profile Connection

Thank You Email #3

Subject: Appreciated Your Time Today

Jane,

The time you took this morning to relate your vast industry knowledge is most appreciated. It will be of great assistance in my job hunt. Visiting directly with you was most uplifting. Your article was the inspiration to have a conversation with you. You inspired me in a new direction for my job search.
I look forward to staying in touch with you and keeping you posted on my progress.

Thanks again for your help,

Full Name: First and Last
Cell Phone Number and City of Current Residence, State
Email Address

Link to Resume Webpage or Resume Document
Linked in Profile Connection

PeoplePoints

New Graduates: The subject line of the email needs to relate the email's content. This addresses the reason for connecting with the person. Do not leave the subject blank. Don't assume your "Thank You" email gets read. Often firewalls block email, or messages are deleted because the recipient doesn't recognize the name. A great tip is to leave a voicemail after work hours but earlier enough in the evening in case the professional's phone has been forwarded to a cell number.

Experienced Professionals: The voicemail should be very short. In it you should briefly state your name and that an email was sent as a thank you. Again this creates a positive impression, together with name repetition and reinforcement, with the new networking connection.

Texting Thank You Notes

An email thank you is recommended over a texted thank you. The thank you email demonstrates graciousness and effort on your behalf, as shown in the previous examples of thank you emails. Complete contact information can be easily saved and forwarded. Be different. Use a text to inform the receiver that your formal thank you is in the receiver's email inbox.

Texting a Thank You

John,
Please check email for my formal thank you.
[your full name]

Best texting tips are to address the recipient by name, followed by a comma as if you were writing a letter, write a very brief text and always end the message with your full name. Your full name needs to be in the text because cell numbers are not always recognized by the recipient. Always use your full name to reinforce recognition and repetition. Abbreviations such as THX should not be used in any digital messaging associated with job hunting.

Complete Email Signatures

The previous signature samples demonstrate the essential elements required for thank you emails and all emails that involve networking. The full information can be easily copied and pasted into a recipient's database for saving, or sent on to another professional in the networking process. Providing full contact information gives the recipient several options with which to connect or reconnect with you, i.e. via a phone call, email, text or LinkedIn. Simple, easy access to contact you is essential.

Line #1 Full Name

Use the full name by which you would like to be known in your professional life. Always sign your full name as name recognition is very important in networking.

Line #2 Cell Number and Geographic Current Residence

For many job candidates, cell phone area codes are not indicative of the area of residence, particularly for students residing temporarily at universities. Knowing the time zones alerts the recipient of your actual physical location for appropriate call times.

List your cell number only for availability and ease of response. One number does not need to be labeled. If you have privacy issues, purchase a prepaid cell phone to be exclusively used in your job search. Do not list your home number or office number as this provides far too many calling options and messages could be lost or not retrieved in a timely manner.

Line #3 Email Address

List your email address, which again should incorporate your full name. Make sure your email address is professional. Eliminate emails with birthdates, cute tag lines or numbers.

Line #4 Resume Document

A link to your resume document page address or web page address enables the recipient to easily save the document and is the most reader-friendly option. Some software databases have the ability to automatically input a word document but not a PDF file.

Line #5 LinkedIn Profile Address

Listing your LinkedIn profile makes it easy for the recipient to immediately click on and view your profile. By listing both a resume document address and LinkedIn profile address, the recipient has two opportunities to view your career experience.

PeoplePoints

New Graduates: Make a complete automatic signature for all your professional emails throughout your job hunt and continue this practice during your professional career.

Experienced Professionals: Your signature and cell phone number, followed by your city and state or residence, will indicate the time zone in which you reside despite what the area code of your cell phone indicates. This allows the recipient to make calls at an appropriate time.

Track Contacts

Contact Management Software is the best way to keep track of new and previous contacts. Contact Management Software is often referred to as CRM. This software is relevant not only to job networking but to the rest of your career as it will help you successfully track and maintain relationships. This will prove to be easier to use in searching for a job than referring to a tracking spreadsheet.

CRM users can access stored information and are provided with integrated tools for connecting with contacts. Entry fields in CRM software include contact information, email integration, records of interactions, mobile access, notes, daily schedule, history, activities, calendar integration, company websites, organization of groups, linking contacts, dialing capabilities, documents, relationships and timelines. Most have many more fields than those listed here.

Software packages include Sage Act, Oncontact, Salesforce, Relenta, Prophet, Contact Plus, Maximizer CRM, Chaos Intellect and FullContact. Study these CRM options and visit with software sales staff to determine which one is the best fit for you personally. Be sure to ask about the cost of upgrades and renewals.

PeoplePoints

New Graduates: You will find a good CRM software package can be used throughout your professional career. It is a valuable tool for sales professionals, but its use is not limited to sales purposes. It will be the best investment for tracking your job hunt and will prove more effective than developing spreadsheets.

Experienced Professionals: It will be no surprise if you find yourself using CRM for family and friends. It is a great way to track changes addresses, major events, birthdays, anniversaries and many more items that you may not be able to store on a smartphone.

Stay Connected

Networking for a job is not a one-time event. You need to continue to keep in touch with contacts even if it is not convenient. The word "work" is part of "network". If you choose to have a network, make sure you are working it for continual growth with new contacts and long-term relationships.

Now is the time to continue to nurture your newly-built job network so it becomes your professional business network for your entire career. Your new permanent part-time job is to continually reconnect with your contacts.

If you promised to keep certain contacts informed of your progress, be sure to follow up in doing so. Once you give your promise in any networking situation, keep it. In the future you will be surprised how your nurtured network can assist you in all aspects of your career.

Invest in your network and create a bond of goodwill. Create a history of shared interest.

Here are a few suggestions on how to stay connected with your new contacts:

One: Send interesting industry articles. Create Internet alerts for articles and be selective about the ones you share with your individual networking contacts.

Two: Inform your contacts about your job search. Send a personalized email when you have secured a new position informing them of your new business contact information.

Three: Offer to do things for your contacts on a professional level. This might include assistance with endorsements, referrals, introductions, encouragement, critiques and guidance nurture networks.

PeoplePoints

New Graduates: Stay professional and keep personal social networking with friends and family both separate and private from your professional network on LinkedIn.

Experienced Professionals: Follow your contacts on LinkedIn with their permission.

This will allow for additional notes of congratulations on promotions, new positions etc. Send notes outside of LinkedIn whenever possible to show extra effort and initiative.

Author's Note

Thank you for purchasing **Network for a Job.**

Numerous job candidates have contacted me throughout the years frustrated because their job hunt was not progressing. My first question was: "With whom have you spoken?" Next I named various professionals that would be helpful to their job hunt. The usual comments were: "I had not thought about contacting them."

The challenges as a solo contingency recruiter are similar to job candidates. Both of us need great referrals and those referrals best come through networking. Ask the right people the right questions and you gain access to private firsthand information essential to uncover job opportunities.

This book has been ten years in the making. I diligently documented the professionals whom I contacted for candidate referrals and hiring managers referrals to gain recruitment contracts. Along the way I learned private firsthand information is how to achieve the goals of referrals.

It has been my pleasure to share with you the PeopleHirePeople® process for building a job-specific network.

I encourage you to write a review on Amazon and I will personally review each one.

For additional job hunt information, activities and articles please go to my website: www. peoplehirepeople.com.